T0193394

Noah's Ark

Written and Illustrated
by Gwenn Huot

Moose
Happenings,

To order additional copies of this book, contact:
Xlibris
844-714-8691
www.Xlibris.com
Orders@Xlibris.com

ISBN: Softcover 978-1-4363-6840-7
         EBook 978-1-6641-4911-3

Print information available on the last page

Rev. date: 12/18/2020

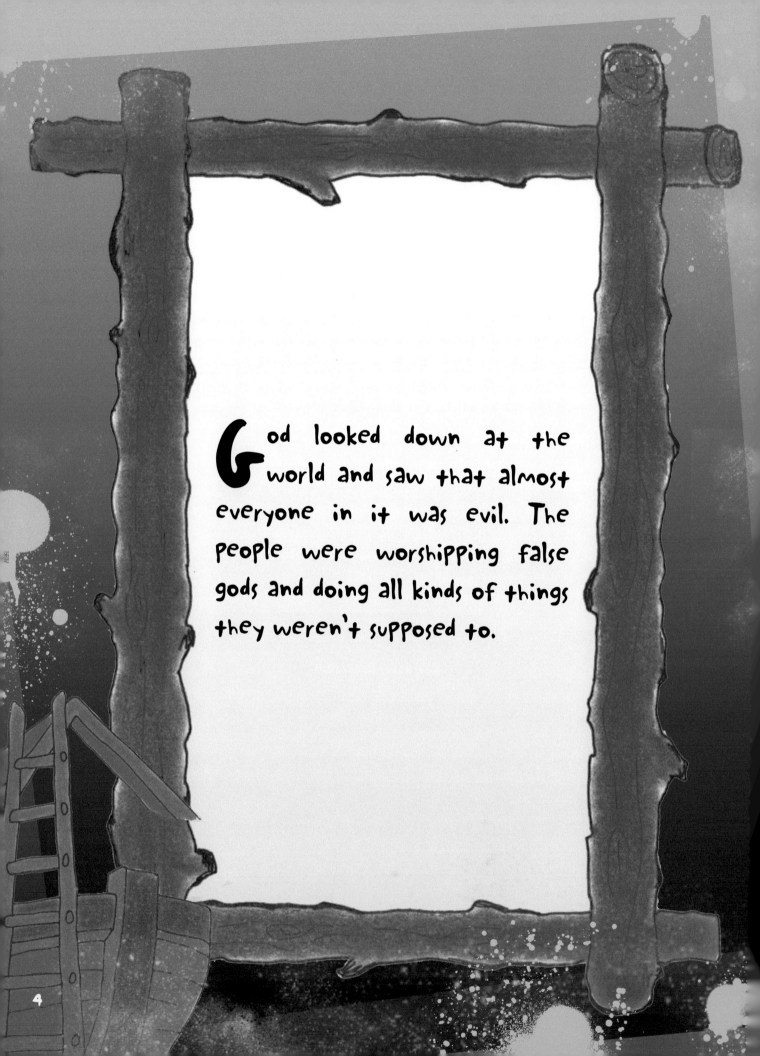

God looked down at the world and saw that almost everyone in it was evil. The people were worshipping false gods and doing all kinds of things they weren't supposed to.

Noah and his family were the only ones left who still loved God. So, God told Noah to build a boat big enough to fit his family into, along with two of every animal. God wanted to flood the earth with water and let Noah and his family start over.

People came from all over to laugh at **Noah** and his family because it had never rained before.

It took Noah 100 years to build the ark. That's a long time!

It rained for 40 days and 40 nights. The whole earth was flooded. It took many months for the water to go down.

After the rain stopped, Noah sent a raven out to see if it would come back or not. There was no land dry enough, so the bird came back.

The second time, Noah sent
a dove and it came back with
an olive leaf.

Now, Noah and his family knew the waters were clearing up.

Finally, it was dry enough to get off the boat. I think everyone was getting seasick.

God sent a beautiful
rainbow as a promise
that He would never
flood the earth again.

So, every time you look in the sky and see a rainbow, you can remember **Noah** and his boat trip.

The animals got off of the boat and made their way through the world to make new homes and multiply their families.

The End

Printed in the United States
By Bookmasters